## DODD, MEAD WONDERS BOOKS

*Wonders of the Mosquito World by Phil Ault*
*Wonders of Animal Migration by Jacquelyn Berrill*
*Wonders of Animal Nurseries by Jacquelyn Berrill*
*Wonders of the Monkey World by Jacquelyn Berrill*
*Wonders of the Arctic by Jacquelyn Berrill*
*Wonders of the Fields and Ponds at Night by Jacquelyn Berrill*
*Wonders of the Woods and Desert at Night by Jacquelyn Berrill*
*Wonders of the World of Wolves by Jacquelyn Berrill*
*Wonders of Alligators and Crocodiles by Wyatt Blassingame*
*Wonders of a Kelp Forest by Joseph E. Brown*
*Wonders of the Pelican World by Joseph J. Cook and Ralph W. Schreiber*
*Wonders Inside You by Margaret Cosgrove*
*Wonders of the Tree World by Margaret Cosgrove*
*Wonders Under a Microscope by Margaret Cosgrove*
*Wonders of Your Senses by Margaret Cosgrove*
*Wonders of the Rivers by Virginia S. Eifert*
*Wonders Beyond the Solar System by Rocco Feravolo*
*Wonders of Gravity by Rocco Feravolo*
*Wonders of Mathematics by Rocco Feravolo*
*Wonders of Sound by Rocco Feravolo*
*Wonders of the World of the Albatross by Harvey I. and Mildred L. Fisher*
*Wonders of the World of Shells by Morris K. Jacobson and William K. Emerson*
*Wonders of Magnets and Magnetism by Owen S. Lieberg*
*Wonders of Measurement by Owen S. Lieberg*
*Wonders of Animal Architecture by Sigmund A. Lavine*
*Wonders of the Bat World by Sigmund A. Lavine*
*Wonders of the Eagle World by Sigmund A. Lavine*
*Wonders of the Fly World by Sigmund A. Lavine*
*Wonders of the Hawk World by Sigmund A. Lavine*
*Wonders of the World of Horses by Sigmund A. Lavine and Brigid Casey*
*Wonders of the Owl World by Sigmund A. Lavine*
*Wonders of the Spider World by Sigmund A. Lavine*
*Wonders of the Dinosaur World by William H. Matthews III*
*Wonders of Fossils by William H. Matthews III*
*Wonders of Sand by Christie McFall*
*Wonders of Snow and Ice by Christie McFall*
*Wonders of Stones by Christie McFall*
*Wonders of Gems by Richard M. Pearl*
*Wonders of Rocks and Minerals by Richard M. Pearl*
*Wonders of Barnacles by Arnold Ross and William K. Emerson*
*Wonders of Hummingbirds by Hilda Simon*

# WONDERS OF
# FROGS AND TOADS

## Wyatt Blassingame

ILLUSTRATED WITH PHOTOGRAPHS

DODD, MEAD & COMPANY · NEW YORK

*Picture Credits:* Wyatt Blassingame, 22; Dick Dickinson, 79; Florida Audubon Society, 2, 15 (bottom), 17, 20, 21 (right), 51, 59, 60, 64, 75 (Dr. Taylor R. Alexander); Florida Game & Fresh Water Fish Commission, 8 (Wallace Hughes), 14, 19 (Frank J. Ligas), 21 (left) (Wallace Hughes), 23 (Frank J. Ligas), 34 (Wallace Hughes), 45 (Lovett Williams), 46 (Lovett Williams), 57 (Wallace Hughes), 62 (Lovett Williams); Florida News Bureau, 10, 52; Edward Greding, Jr., 41, 55; Dr. Victor Hutchison, University of Oklahoma, 48; Nasco-Steinhilber, 15 (top), 26, 28, 29, 30, 54, 78; Gabriel A. Palkuti, 69, 72, 73; Leonard Lee Rue III, 24, 56; Ultrascience, Inc., 43 (Erich L. Gibbs); U. S. Fish and Wildlife Service, 32.

**Library of Congress Cataloging in Publication Data**

Blassingame, Wyatt.
    Wonders of frogs and toads.

    SUMMARY: Text and photographs introduce the physical characteristics and habits of various species of frogs and toads.
    Includes index.
    1. Frogs—Juvenile literature.   2.   Toads—Juvenile literature. [1. Frogs.   2.   Toads]   I. Title.
QL668.E2B513        597'.8        74-25523
ISBN 0-396-07086-8

*For Miss Molly*
*with love*

# ACKNOWLEDGMENTS

For such a short book I need to thank a rather long list of people. Mr. Ben Emmons, Director of the Science Education Division of NASCO, has patiently answered letter after letter, furnished pictures, and referred me to other authorities. Dr. George Nace of the University of Michigan, and Dr. Erich Gibbs, Director of Research and Development of Ultrascience, Inc., have supplied information. Dr. Victor Hutchison of the University of Oklahoma gave me the story and pictures of the Lake Titicaca frog. Mr. Wallace Hughes of *Florida Wildlife* magazine and Betty McDonell of the Florida Audubon Society have been most helpful, along with many others.

Many thanks.

# CONTENTS

1. The First Voice on Earth     9
   *Some Superstitions 11*
2. What Is a Frog and a Toad?     13
   *How Do You Tell a Frog from a Toad? 14*
3. The Frog in Spring     16
   *Courtship 18*
   *The Beginning of Life 24*
4. The Tadpole     27
   *The Fast and the Slow 31*
   *The Big and the Little 34*
   *The Dangers of Tadpole Life 35*
   *Some of the Odd Ones 37*
5. The Frog in Summer     42
   *The Eyes 44*
   *Breathing 47*
   *Ears 50*
   *The Skin Eaters 52*
   *Enemies and Defense 53*
6. Jumping Frogs     58
   *How Smart are Frogs? 63*
7. The Strange and Unusual     66
   *Flying and Fighting 68*
8. Small, Beautiful, and Deadly     71
9. The Friends of Man     77
   Index     80

*A close-up of a bullfrog*

# CHAPTER 1

# THE FIRST VOICE ON EARTH

Around 350 million years ago some strange-looking creatures began, for the first time, to crawl out of the sea onto dry land. This was during what scientists now call the Devonian Period. Life in the sea included both fishes and plants. Along the edge of the seas some plants had taken root and moved slowly inland. There were insects that crawled or flew. But there were no back-boned animals anywhere on land.

This was a time when long spells of dry weather might follow great floods. Then the seas would draw back. Inland ponds and lakes would dry up, leaving the fish to die. It is quite possible that the first backboned animals to move onto land were really trying to stay in the water: as the ponds dried, some creatures managed to struggle across the muddy shallows from one pool to another. Over a period of thousands upon thousands of years some species developed strong fins that could be used for crawling. Their gills changed so they could take oxygen from the air. Eventually some of them came to live part of their lives on land, part in the water.

Animals that live both on land and in the water are now called amphibians. The word actually means "double life": a

9

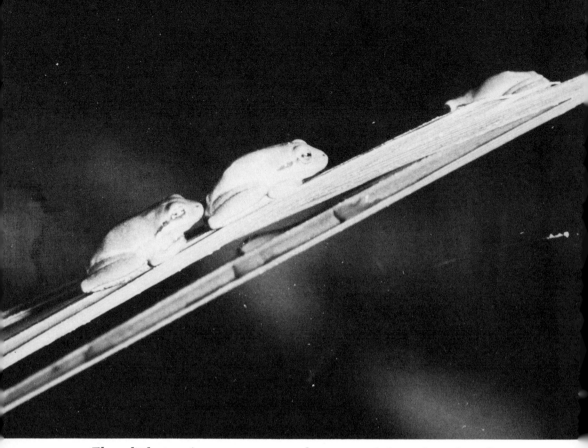

*These little tree frogs are no more than one inch long, but when they begin to sing in chorus, they can be heard a quarter mile or more.*

creature that can—and usually must—live part of its life on land and part in the water.

Among the first amphibians were the direct ancestors of our frogs and toads. Some of them were monsters ten feet long, but some must have looked very much as they do today.

These first frogs came hopping into a world that in many ways must have been very noisy. Volcanoes exploded. Sometimes they created new islands in the sea, and sometimes they blew old ones apart. There were terrific storms, with howling winds, crashing thunder, and the booming of waves. But also there must have been times of eerie quiet. When the storms

10

died and the seas were calm, there was no animal voice anywhere on land to break the silence.

Then the frogs began to croak—the first voiced animal upon the land.

Just how and why these early frogs developed a voice no one can say for sure. Probably it came from that deep, instinctive need of all life to create new life in its own form. Scattered about the prehistoric swamps, each individual searching for food on its own, the male and female frogs needed some way to find one another in order to breed. If the male frog had a voice and the female could hear, they could come together.

As we shall see later, this is the chief use that frogs make of their voices today.

But it is interesting to think, when you hear the singing of frogs on a spring night, that this is the oldest voice upon the earth.

## SOME SUPERSTITIONS

Throughout human history mankind seems to have regarded frogs with a curious mixture of affection, awe, and superstition. Some of the earliest fairy tales are about the handsome prince or beautiful princess who had been changed into a frog. The story is found in many languages from all parts of the world. Nearly always the prince or princess needed love to be returned to human form.

In Malaya one brightly colored frog is thought to be sacred. It is carried in religious processions—seated in its own chair.

African natives believe that a certain frog not only can foretell rain, but that it can either cause or prevent rain. This naturally makes it sacred to farmers. If a farmer accidentally digs up a rain frog, he carefully replaces it in the ground, then adds a little of his own food as an apology for disturbing the frog.

11

During the Middle Ages both medical doctors and witch doctors used dried frog skins in their medicines. In Shakespeare's play *Macbeth* there is a scene where three witches mix a magic potion in a boiling cauldron. As they do, the first chants:

> Round about the cauldron go;
> In the poison'd entrails throw.
> Toad, that under cold stone
> Days and nights hast thirty-one
> Swelter'd venom sleeping got,
> Boil thou first i' the charmed pot.

Then the second witch adds her part to the magic brew:

> Fillet of a fenny snake,
> In the cauldron boil and bake;
> Eye of newt, and toe of frog,
> Wool of bat, and tongue of dog,
>
> •     •     •
>
> For a charm of powerful trouble,
> Like a hell-broth boil and bubble.

Even today many people believe that handling a frog or toad can cause warts. Probably this is because most toads are pretty warty themselves. Doctors don't fully understand what does cause warts to appear or disappear. But they do know one thing for sure: handling a toad doesn't have anything to do with it.

In recent years, as we shall see later, frogs have been the subject of much serious, scientific study. In fact, very few animals have added as much to human knowledge as has the frog. They are not only interesting little creatures, they are well worth knowing something about.

# CHAPTER 2

# WHAT IS A FROG
# AND A TOAD?

Strangely, this is a question both easy and difficult to answer.

Frogs and toads are found around the world, on every continent except Antarctica. There are about 2,600 different species —a hundred or so in North America—but there are new ones still being discovered. In fact, there are so many species, and some so different from others, that it's difficult to make a statement that will apply to all of them.

There are frogs that can sit in a teaspoon with room left over, and there are frogs the size of small dogs. Some live in trees and some prefer holes in the ground. They not only come in a wide variety of colors, but almost every frog or toad can change its color. Even so, if you take a good, long look at a frog or toad— just any one, anywhere in the world—the chances are that the next time you see one, no matter what kind, you can say, "That looks like a frog to me."

Because, somehow, they do *look* alike. They sit hunched up. Their back legs are longer than their front legs. In fact, their back legs have four joints, the front legs three. This gives most of them great jumping power. They sit with these back legs folded up beneath, behind, or alongside them. They have big heads, no necks, and their bulging eyes make them look as if

*A salamander, member of the order Caudata*

they are pondering some very important problem. Gray, green, or rainbow colored, in trees, ponds, or under rocks, they still somehow look alike.

This, of course, is not a very scientific definition. Scientifically, frogs and toads, as mentioned earlier, are amphibians, and today scientists divide all living amphibians into three groups, or orders.

One order, Gynmophiona, is composed of the caecilians— legless, blind, wormlike creatures that live mostly underground in the tropics. Few people have seen them and even fewer know much about them.

Then there are the salamanders, the order Caudata. These have legs and tails; they look like lizards and are often called that, although they are not true lizards.

And there is the order Salientia or Anura; it doesn't seem to matter which name is used. Salientia means "the jumping ones"; Anura means "tailless," and both names fit the frogs and toads. So they are amphibians with legs but without tails.

### HOW DO YOU TELL A FROG FROM A TOAD?

In many cases this is fairly easy. Frogs, as a rule, have a smooth, moist skin while the skin of toads feels dry and rough. Most toads also have a lot of warts. At least, they look like warts

14

*The marine toad, Bufo marinus, is the giant of all toads. In its native South America, it sometimes reaches a length of 8½ inches.*

though many of them are really glands. The hind legs of frogs are usually longer and stronger than those of toads, so frogs are more apt to jump where toads hop. And most adult frogs stay close to water, while toads may be found miles away.

There are some species where even the scientists argue over whether it is a true frog, a true toad, or a very close relative. The differences are too small to trouble most persons.

Scientists have a Latin name for each individual species, or they may use the words anuran or salientian to cover them all. But in English, frog and toad are the only names we have for tailless amphibians. In fact, the word frog is often used, like the scientific anuran, for all species. That's how it will be in this book much of the time.

*The bullfrog—Rana catesbeiana—is the biggest of all North American frogs. Note the webs between the toes that make it such an excellent swimmer.*

# CHAPTER 3

# THE FROG IN SPRING

There is an ancient expression that, "It rained so hard it poured down frogs." And it is true that after a heavy spring rain frogs may often be seen hopping all over the place. Almost 2,000 years ago a man named Atheneau wrote that it once rained so many frogs "that houses and roads have been full with them; and at first for some days the inhabitants, endeavoring to kill them and shutting up their houses, endured the pests." But the frogs kept pouring down, and the people, Atheneau wrote, "could not make use of any water, nor put their feet on the ground for the heaps of frogs that were everywhere, and they were annoyed by the smell of those that had died. They fled the country."

Atheneau wasn't there when this happened and the odds are the number of frogs got exaggerated in the telling. But whatever the number, it is almost certain they did not fall with the rain.

True, a tornado or any great storm may suck up frogs and other objects from one place and dump them in another. But a tornado can only pick up what it passes over, and it's not likely to get any great number of frogs. The adult frogs and toads that suddenly appear after spring rains come from the other direction. Actually, they pop up out of the ground or from the bottom of ponds.

16

*This is a barking tree frog —Hyla gratiosa. In summer, this frog may be heard singing from the tops of tall pine trees, but in winter it has been found buried four feet underground.*

To understand this it is necessary to know something about the frog's life cycle.

Frogs and toads—all amphibians—are cold-blooded animals. That means the frog has no way to create a body temperature of its own, as does a human being. So the frog's temperature is always very close to that of the air or earth or water around it. If the weather gets too hot and the frog cannot find a cool, moist spot—frogs dry out in a hurry if the air is dry—it will die. This is the reason you will rarely see a frog or toad hopping about the yard on a very hot, dry day.

On the other hand, frogs cannot stand intense cold either. As the temperature drops, they dive to the bottom of the pond and bury themselves in the mud. Toads are more likely to bury themselves on land, where the earth is moist and cool. There, as it gets colder and colder, the animal's breathing, heartbeat, and circulation, get slower and slower. This is called hibernation and the frog may live like this, motionless, in a kind of sleep, all winter. At such times no frog will be visible above the ground. If the place where the frog is buried should actually freeze, the frog freezes also, and dies. Instinct, however, usually directs it to a safe spot.

Then comes the spring. The weather begins to warm, and with it the spot where the frog or toad is buried. A heavy spring

17

rain softens and warms the earth still more. The amphibian's heart beats a little faster, and it needs more air. It awakes and starts for the surface. And since a good spring rain may fetch up practically all the frogs and toads in an area, they may seem to have rained from the sky.

## COURTSHIP

You would think that when a frog pops up from wherever it has spent the winter, it would be hungry and its first thought would be of food. But it is not. The one overwhelming drive of the adult frog when it first awakes is to mate and reproduce other frogs.

Although the first amphibians crawled out of the water many millions of years ago, they returned to the water to breed. And in most cases, their direct descendants, the amphibians of today, must do the same. Their eggs must be laid in water, and the young must spend the first part of their lives in water. (There are exceptions, and some of these will be mentioned later.)

Now here is a strange thing. A toad may have spent the winter buried in a garden or in the basement of a farmhouse where the ground stays comparatively warm. With spring and the moisture of rain in the air, it comes to the surface. The nearest pond may be a half mile, a mile, or even farther away. But the toad will head for it, hopping slowly, steadily, driven by the same instinct that has driven its ancestors for millions upon millions of years.

How does the toad know in which direction to hop? Does it remember where it came from the previous year? Or does it have some way of sensing water far beyond its vision? No one knows for sure. Nor does anyone know if toads, year after year, return to the same pond in which they were born. Perhaps they do. Naturalists working with frogs have carried them a mile or

18

more from their home pond to release. Many of them head straight home again, even though there may be other ponds nearby.

However they find their way, once they have awakened in the spring, frogs and toads quickly begin to gather around water. Depending on species and location this may be a large lake, a pond, even a puddle or roadside ditch. Often a dozen or more species will gather at the same spot. Usually the males arrive first. And now on the warm, spring nights the voice of the frog is heard in the land. There are some toads that actually begin to croak with the first touch of warm rain, while they are still underground.

People in the South used to say that the little frogs cried in high, thin voices, "How deep? How deep?" And the big bull-frogs answered in their deep, bass voices, "Belly deep. Belly deep." Actually, every species has its own distinctive voice. The

*Male (lower) and female (upper) pig frogs—Rana grylio*

*The spring peeper, Hyla crucifer, a small tree frog and one of the very first to begin calling in the spring. Found in eastern United States and Canada, it is about one inch long.*

pig frog does sound almost exactly like a pig grunting; the cricket frog sounds like a cricket; the Florida gopher frog sounds like a man snoring; but the pine woods tree frog and many toads have lovely, trilling, birdlike voices. If you ride at night along a country road, the voices, all mixed together, may pour through your car windows in great waves of sound, fading, then swelling again as you pass one roadside marsh after another.

In most species only the males sing and they do this, oddly enough, with both their mouths and nostrils closed. This way

*This little tree frog is singing, calling for a mate. It does this with both the mouth and nostrils closed, pumping the air back and forth from vocal sac to lungs across the vocal chords. The vocal sac, made of elastic skin under the frog's neck, can swell out bigger than its head.*

they can pump the same air back and forth across their vocal cords. Also, most species have an elastic skin sac below the mouth, or they may have two elastic sacs, one on each side of the mouth. These swell out like great bubble gum balloons as the frog sings. They increase the sound the same way a drum does.

Probably the best known frog voice in the United States is that of the spring peeper, one of the very first to call in the spring. The male is no bigger than the last joint of your thumb, but its vocal sac will swell until it just about doubles its size. Some people say the peeper sounds like sleigh bells; some say it's more like a tin whistle. Either way, it's an amazing noise to come from so small a creature. When a hundred or more are singing in chorus, they can be heard a half a mile away.

The steady calling of the male frogs attracts the females. And since every species has its own call, the female cricket frogs are attracted to the male cricket frogs, the female green tree frogs to the male green tree frogs. Now and then, however, things do get a bit mixed up. Where the species are very closely related to one another, the calls are usually very similar. Apparently the frogs themselves can't always tell one from another. So there are cases of cross breeding, as when a barking tree frog may mate with a green tree frog.

*Left: A green tree frog,* Hyla cinerea. *Right: Sometimes two different but very similar species of frogs will crossbreed. The offspring is called a hybrid. This hybrid is probably a cross between a green tree frog and a barking tree frog.*

*Raccoons may be cute to people, but they are an enemy of the frogs.*

Normally frogs have good night vision, but in mating they do not seem to make much use of it. Depending on his species, the male may be calling from the pond with just his head above the surface, or from on the bank. The small tree frogs may sing from bushes or blades of grass nearby. Wherever he is, if he hears or sees another frog close by, he jumps on its back and clasps it around the body with his arms.

Quite often this may be another male. Then the second male makes a loud snorting noise. Apparently this means, "Are you crazy or something?" With no answer the first frog immediately lets go, jumps off, and begins to sing again.

Most frogs, both male and female, also have a distress call. Caught by a raccoon or snake, or even picked up roughly by hand, the frog may give a short, startling scream. It makes this scream with the mouth wide open and it may be so startling that the coon or snake may drop its victim in surprise.

In the south where the weather stays warm much of the time some frogs have a longer breeding season than in the north. Yet even in the north there are times when frogs can be heard croaking away after the mating season is over. Some naturalists believe frogs use this method of claiming ownership of a certain amount of territory. The frog may be saying, "This spot is mine; there's just food enough here for me, and the rest of you find a place of your own." Also, it's possible that frogs may sing sometimes just for the fun of it.

Normally, however, the voice of the frog is a mating call. When it leads the male and female together, the male climbs on the female's back, clasping her around the body with his short, thick arms. Scientifically this is called *amplexus.* Since the female is the larger, she can carry the male without difficulty until she is ready to lay her eggs. This may be within a few minutes, or it may be a few days or even weeks. During this time the female will hop or swim about, feeding and finding the right spot to place her eggs. As the eggs issue from her body, the male fertilizes them with his sperm.

The number of eggs, where they are placed, and what happens after that varies greatly with the species.

*Pig frogs in breeding posture or amplexus*

Some species of frogs or toads may lay as many as 35,000 eggs at one time. Others may lay only a dozen or so. But the size of the frog usually has nothing to do with the number of its eggs. Nor does the size of the individual egg depend on the size of the frog. Some species that never get to be more than two inches long have eggs as big as the tip of your little finger, while bullfrogs, that may get to be eight inches long or more, have eggs no bigger than the head of a pin.

On a rough average, frogs and toads will lay about 5,000 eggs at a time. Depending on the species, these may be in long, spaghetti-like strings, often fastened to underwater plants, or

*Eggs of the American toad*

they may float on the surface in clusters. Either way, the eggs are coated with a jelly-like substance that helps to protect them.

Once in the water this jelly quickly begins to swell. Soon the mass of eggs may be far larger than the female who laid it: the bullfrog's eggs may easily cover five square feet.

A newly laid egg is round and semitransparent. Part of it is dark colored, part a pale white or yellow. The dark part is called the animal pole, and this holds the almost invisible speck of life that will eventually become a frog. All living things, even something as small as the spot inside a frog's egg, must eat in order to exist. So the lighter colored part of the egg, called the vegetable pole, holds the food.

Life inside this tiny egg will develop much as it does with all animals, from worms to human beings. And because the frog egg is semitransparent, it offers us a better chance to watch and understand this miraculous development than does any other form of life.

Almost as soon as it is laid and fertilized, the egg begins to change. As new cells develop, the shape changes from round to a sort of lopsided oval. At the same time the speck of life in the top part of the egg is growing. It grows a head and a pointed tail. It grows gills like those of a fish for breathing. Now it is big enough to be seen clearly with the naked eye. A dark groove marks the developing backbone. It begins to wiggle. A mass of frog eggs at the point of hatching may seem to shimmer, to tremble with the life seething inside it.

The larva—as the life inside the egg is called—has now consumed most of the food from the vegetable pole. Also, it has used up most of the oxygen inside the egg. It must break free if it is to continue to live.

For such a tiny creature this seems impossible. But along with its gills and tail it has developed glands on the tip of its snout. These discharge a secretion that softens, then dissolves the egg

*Tadpoles which will soon develop into frogs*

case. At the same time the mass of jelly that has protected the eggs is breaking up. The larva comes wiggling out into a watery world.

The time needed for all this to happen varies not only with the species, but with the weather. If the weather is warm, some species may hatch in two days or even less. If the weather is cold, it may take three weeks or so. Whenever it happens, the larva, free of its egg and jelly, is now called a tadpole or "polliwog."

26

CHAPTER 4

# THE TADPOLE

To watch a human baby grow into an adult takes a long time. Nor is there any startling change in shape after the child is born. Mainly, the baby just seems to get bigger. The same thing is true for most of the animals we commonly see. But a tadpole is something else altogether. Even while still in its egg this tiny speck of life was visible. Now hatched and on its own, it looks nothing like the frog or toad it will become. And all these miraculous changes are clearly visible. If kept in an aquarium or even a glass jar, we can watch the tadpole change day by day.

Just out of its egg case the tadpole doesn't have much shape at all. It looks as much like a tiny bit of earthworm as anything else. Some species hang up right near the surface, others lie on the bottom, or cling to bits of grass. Apparently worn out by the struggle to escape from the egg, they are now motionless, resting.

Usually within two days, and sometimes even quicker, changes appear. The gills grow until they may be easily seen. The tadpole begins to swim about and feed.

For its size, the tadpole is truly a champion eater. When it's not eating, it's looking for something to eat. The food, of course, is small and the tadpole needs a lot of it. Most of the food at

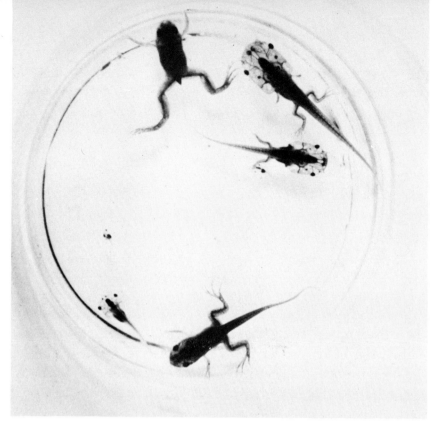

*This shows the various stages of a tadpole's life. The smallest one has just been born—or become free of its egg. This happened approximately seventy-two hours after the egg was fertilized. Note how transparent is the skin of the younger tadpoles, so that various organs and blood vessels may be seen. The oldest, about eleven weeks, has almost completed its metamorphosis into a frog.*

this stage is made up of tiny bits of plant life. However, if the tadpole comes on an animal small enough to eat, it gobbles that down also.

The tadpole's busy mouth looks somewhat like that of a parrot. At least there is a horny beak like a parrot's beak. In most species there are also teeth, too small to be seen without a magnifying glass. Under a glass they look more like the rough parts of a file than teeth. Using both its beak and teeth, the tadpole scrapes minute bits of algae from rocks, grass, and anything else it finds floating in the water.

The tadpole uses its mouth for breathing as well as eating. To do this, it takes water in through the mouth and passes it over the gills. The gills take oxygen from the water much as our lungs take oxygen from the air. Then the water passes out of a hole called the spiracle, or spiraculum. This is usually in the tadpole's side, but in some species it's in the belly.

Eating away, the tadpole grows rapidly. But even as the tadpole grows, its gills quit growing. A bit of skin, called the opercular fold, grows over the gills. Now enclosed in the body, they begin to change from gills to lungs. More and more the tadpole needs to take oxygen from the air rather than from the water. It begins to pop to the surface to breathe, then down again.

Getting bigger, the tadpole changes its diet from almost all vegetables to almost all animal matter. And with this comes another curious internal change. Herbivores—animals that eat grass and vegetable matter—need longer intestines to digest their food than do carnivores—animals that eat meat. As the tadpole changes from a vegetable to a meat diet, its intestines grow shorter.

At the same time other and still stranger changes are taking place. Along the tadpole's sides faint bulges appear where hind legs are growing. Finally first one leg, then the other, will break

*At nine weeks the legs of this laboratory-raised African clawed frog begin to develop. Here one has broken free and shows clearly. The skin at the head of the tadpole is transparent and some organs can be seen. At this stage, the tadpole does not swim as well as it did two weeks earlier. The penny is to illustrate size. This is as big as the tadpole will get.*

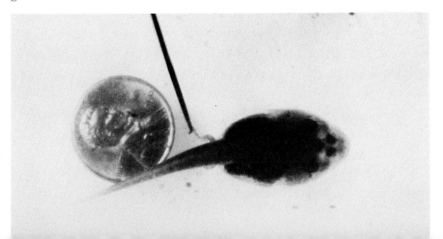

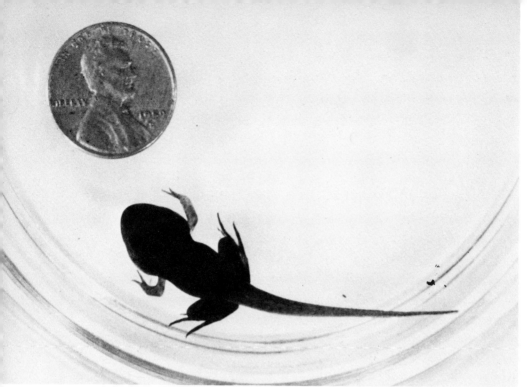

*Above: The tadpole of the African clawed frog at ten weeks. Now all four legs have appeared and the back legs are well developed. The head is definitely froglike, and internal lungs are replacing the gills. Below: After twelve weeks this African clawed frog has almost completed its metamorphosis. The tail is almost absorbed, leaving only a stub. It no longer breathes underwater. By this time the frog's diet has changed from vegetable to animal matter.*

free of the skin. The tadpole continues to use its tail for swimming, the new, small legs trailing downward.

Front legs appear under the skin, then break free. The hind legs grow longer and stronger and the tadpole begins to use them to swim instead of its tail.

At this time, if a tadpole loses an arm or leg in an accident, it will grow a new one. But if this should happen later, to a fully grown frog, the limb won't be replaced.

About the time a tadpole stops using its tail for swimming, it also stops eating. Instead, it now feeds off its own tail. To do this it does not turn around and bite itself: rather, the tail, little by little, is absorbed into the tadpole's body. While this happens, the tadpole's body may, or may not, get slightly bigger. But always its legs strengthen. Its eyes begin to bulge. Its mouth has already lost its beaklike look. Finally the tail becomes a mere stub, then nothing at all.

One day a small but complete frog comes hopping out of the water to take up its life on land.

THE FAST AND THE SLOW

This change from tadpole to frog or toad is called *metamorphosis*. How long it takes depends on both weather and species. It may be anywhere from a few days to as much as three years.

Bullfrogs are among the biggest of our frogs and slowest to metamorphose. In the south this change will usually take place within one year. But in the north ponds and lakes do not become warm until later in the spring, so the bullfrogs are later in mating. In the cool water the eggs hatch more slowly. As the water chills with winter, the still immature tadpole will hibernate just as the mature frog will do later. So the complete change from tadpole to frog may take two or even three years.

31

*This is a spadefoot toad. When frightened, it will use the sharp edges of its feet to shovel out the dirt behind it so fast that the toad seems almost to dive, rear end first, into the ground.*

If the bullfrog is slow to metamorphose, some of the western spadefoot toads are real speed demons. By the time one tadpole has turned into a baby bullfrog, the spadefoot tadpole would be an old man—or at least getting along in years. The reason for this goes back to the habitat in which each lives.

The bullfrog makes its home in ponds or swamps where there is water all or most of the year. The spadefoot lives in areas so dry they are almost desert at times. This would be impossible if it were not for the spadefoot's spadefoot. Along the inner edges of its hind feet this toad has tough, horny rims that it can use like a spade. With this it can shovel dirt so fast that the spadefoot seems to sink, rear end first, into the ground almost as fast as a bullfrog can dive headfirst into water. When the spadefoot finds a moist spot in the earth, it stays there much of the time. Even in summer it rarely comes out except at night when the air is damp. For this reason many people never see a spadefoot toad, even though many of them may live close by.

In the desert-like country where some spadefoot toads live, finding water in which to lay eggs is a problem. Even when water is found, it is likely to be a small pool that will dry up within days or weeks. So in nature's miraculous way the spadefoot has adapted itself. Some species—there are several, differing only slightly—lay eggs that will hatch within two days. Within another ten days the tadpole changes its gills for lungs, grows legs, absorbs its tail, and comes hopping onto dry land.

Yet even within ten days—and some of the spadefoot toads need five or six weeks to metamorphose—the desert pool may be drying up. And here is another curious thing. (It sometimes seems that everything about frogs and toads is rather curious.) Under normal circumstances every tadpole is on its own from the moment it breaks from its egg case. But as the water in their small pool gets lower and lower, the spadefoot tadpoles band together. They lash their tiny tails back and forth. This makes a small depression in the bottom of the pool and here the water may stand a few hours longer than elsewhere. In the rapid metamorphosis of the spadefoot toad an hour or two may mean the difference between life and death.

This banding together of the tadpoles has another benefit. In the small desert pools, food may be very scarce. And since the spadefoot lays eggs by the thousands, there may be a great swarm of tadpoles. Lashing their tails, they not only deepen the pool, they stir up the mud on the bottom. This contains bits of vegetable and dried animal matter on which the tadpoles can feed.

Despite this, the desert pool may dry up before the metamorphosis is complete. The tadpoles die, and their dried bodies become part of the bottom. Then next spring the rains come again. The pool fills; the adult toads lay eggs that hatch; and the new tadpoles feed unknowingly on the remains of those that died the year before.

The diet is good for them. Naturalists working with spade-foot toads have learned that when tadpoles are raised in the same pool where many died the year before, the new crop grows much faster than usual.

### THE BIG AND THE LITTLE

Like the size of the egg, the size of a tadpole is no proof of the size frog it will become. In Trinidad and in parts of South America there is a frog now called the paradoxical frog. For many years the frog itself was unknown, but the native Indians knew the tadpole well. It grew to be a foot long; some people said even bigger. The natives caught them in nets, even on hooks and lines like fish, and ate them happily.

When scientists first heard of these giant tadpoles, they figured the mature frogs must be even bigger. Expeditions went to Trinidad and the Amazon. They had no trouble catching the tadpoles, but not the frogs. There simply didn't seem to be a wild frog that matched this great tadpole.

Then some of the tadpoles were raised in an aquarium where the naturalists could watch. They saw the long tail of the tad-

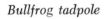

*Bullfrog tadpole*

pole shrink, as it was absorbed by the maturing frog. But the frog itself got no bigger. When finally the whole tail was gone the frog was only two and one-half to three inches long.

On the other hand, the bullfrog tadpole is rarely more than five or six inches long. But the full grown frog may be as much as seven or eight inches. (This measurement is from the tip of the snout to the end of the body. In scientific measurements the legs are not counted. With its hind legs outstretched, a bullfrog may well be twelve inches long or more.)

All of which will help explain why:

> The tadpole is very strange
> From day to day you'll see it change.
> Though big of head and long of tail
> It doesn't grow to be a whale.
> Instead of bigger, it smaller grows
> While adding arms and legs and toes,
> So when it leaves the water to hit the road
> It's not a tadpole, it's a toad.

### THE DANGERS OF TADPOLE LIFE

Frogs and toads, as mentioned before, will lay an average of about 5,000 eggs at a time, and some species lay many more. If even half of these lived to be adults, we'd all be up to our hips in frogs. But the life of the egg and tadpole is not an easy one.

When the female frog picks the spot to lay her eggs she is guided by instinct. But instinct is not proof against all the dangers that threaten the eggs. The weather may be drier than usual. The pond shrinks and the underwater plants to which some eggs were attached are left high on the bank. Even floating eggs may be left dry. Then the sun beating on them destroys the life inside.

35

Nor are the eggs that remain in the water free from danger. All life feeds on life. The larvae of water beetles and the nymphs of dragonflies eat the eggs hungrily. Leeches and water worms eat the eggs. Even the hungry tadpoles that hatched a few days earlier will gobble their unhatched relatives.

For the tadpole that does wiggle its way out of the egg, danger is just beginning. Fish that rarely eat the unhatched eggs, devour the tadpoles by thousands. Wading birds, snakes, and turtles feed on them. Even the parent frogs turn cannibal if a tadpole swims in front of them. An insect called the giant water bug hangs upside down in the underwater grass where the tadpoles swim. About two inches long, it is not as big as some tadpoles; but if a tadpole the right size swims near, the water bug grabs it with powerful arms. It stabs its beak into the tadpole's body and sucks out the juices.

Perhaps the most curious of all the tadpole's enemies is not an animal at all. It's a plant, called bladderwort—a revolting name if ever I heard one. Despite its name and its strange nature of feeding on animal life, it's a rather pretty plant with small white, or pink, or purple blossoms. It floats in the water and along the edges of its leaves are tiny sacs, each one fitted with a trap door that is fastened at the top but open at the bottom. Around the edge of each sac are four tiny bristles.

Waiting for food, the bladderwort's sacs are squeezed shut. But when a tadpole, or some other bit of life touches one of the bristles, the sac suddenly opens. This sucks in water—and the tadpole with it. At the same instant the trap door swings shut. The tadpole is caught inside, and the bladderwort's digestive juices turn it into food.

Bladderworts and insects together, however, cannot equal man-made pollution in destroying tadpoles, as well as other forms of life. Chemical and industrial wastes may poison the water or deprive it of oxygen. Oil scum may make it impossible to breathe.

36

No one really knows what percentage of frog eggs ever hatch or how many tadpoles ever turn into frogs. But some naturalists have estimated that if a frog laid 20,000 eggs, about 1,000 of them would eventually become frogs.

Even this figure may be high. But if ten frogs and toads lay 20,000 eggs each in the same pool at about the same time, as often happens, a vast number of these may metamorphose at approximately the same time. Many baby frogs are no bigger than houseflies. If all these come hopping out of the pond about the same time the whole earth may seem covered with tiny, leaping objects. And when this happens after a hard summer rain, then no wonder some people believe it rained frogs.

### SOME OF THE ODD ONES

As already described, the great majority of anurans—tailless amphibians—lay eggs in the water, which hatch into tadpoles, which in turn metamorphose into frogs or toads. But when you have 2,000 or more species, it's almost certain that some are not going to follow the rules.

The greenhouse frog lives in the southeastern United States and gets its name because it is often found in greenhouses or even in flowerpots. Fully grown it is never more than one and one-fourth inches long, so a flowerpot can make a happy home. Reddish brown in color, it may have two pink or orange stripes down its sides, or it may be splotched with dark brown and no stripes at all.

Wherever it lives, the greenhouse frog has no need to go looking for a pond to lay its eggs. Instead it chooses some damp spot under leaves or between rocks. The eggs are rather large for so small a frog, but there are only one or two dozen of them, each wrapped singly in its bag of jelly.

Within a day or two a tiny larva can be seen inside the egg. In another day or two it takes on tadpole shape. But the tadpole does not break free of its egg. There would be no water for it to swim in, and with only gills for breathing, it would die. With surprising speed the tadpole, still inside the egg, begins its metamorphosis. The legs and arms begin to grow, the gills are covered over. But with the gills covered and still inside the egg it must get oxygen in some way. This tadpole's tail is long for its size, thin, and with many blood vessels. These blood vessels absorb the oxygen from the vegetable pole of the egg. And so the tadpole breathes through its tail at the same time the tail is being absorbed into the body.

Then comes the time when the tadpole, having changed into a frog while still in the egg, must break free. To do this it doesn't use glands on the end of its snout. It doesn't have any. It does have something called an egg tooth, a real tooth at the front of the upper jaw. With this it cuts its way out of the egg: a complete frog no more than one-fifth of an inch long.

A close relative of the greenhouse frog is the barking frog, so-called because some people think its voice sounds like that of a dog. This is not the small barking tree frog found in the southeast. This one lives in Central Texas and parts of Mexico, often in caves or very rocky areas, and grows to be three times as big as its little greenhouse relative. The barking frog female lays her eggs in damp cracks between the rocks or in caves, then she forgets them and goes hopping off after food. But not the male. For 25 to 35 days, as long as it takes the baby frogs to metamorphose completely inside the eggs, the male stands guard. If the weather turns dry he dampens the eggs with urine and guards them against insects.

Of all the frogs in North America the barking frog is thought to be the only one that guards its eggs.

In other parts of the world there are frogs and toads that make their North American relatives, even the papa barking frog, look like very careless parents. Take the Surinam toad that lives along the Amazon and Orinoco rivers in South America.

Few toads are beautiful, but the Surinam is undoubtedly one of the ugliest to be found anywhere. It looks as if somebody had stepped on it, squashing it flat. Its skin is mud colored, making it almost invisible on muddy river banks. The nose is long and pointed, the fingers abnormally long, and the big webbed feet look as if it were wearing snowshoes.

Even so, the Surinam toad is a good mother—up to a point. As her eggs are laid—single, tiny, round balls—the male uses his body to push them up on the female's back, each into a small pocket in her skin. After sixty or so eggs are laid and in place on the female's back, the male goes his carefree way. The female remains quiet for several hours. During this time the skin on her back swells to cover the eggs. This makes her look fatter and uglier than usual, but doesn't trouble her otherwise. She goes about her business, eating and swimming, apparently unaware of what she is carrying. The young develop into tadpoles and then into frogs still inside the eggs, just as do the greenhouse frogs. And then one day a whole batch of little Surinam toads wiggle free and jump down off their mother's back. When this happens in an aquarium, it's best to remove the mother. Otherwise she may casually eat her own offspring.

The midwife toad, a native of Central Europe, does things somewhat differently. Most frogs and toads mate at night, often in the water, but the midwife usually mates during daylight and always on land. The female lays her eggs in long strings. The male fertilizes them as they emerge, then carefully pushes his legs through the tangle of eggs until they are wrapped securely about his thighs. At this point the female forgets the whole business. The male, with the eggs wrapped around him, goes to his underground burrow. After dark he comes out to take his eggs for a swim, or he may simply go for a hop through the dew-wet grass. However it is done, he keeps the eggs damp and with daylight goes back underground.

The male midwife follows this routine until he knows by

instinct that the eggs are ready to hatch into tadpoles. At this time the wet grass will not do. He finds a pond and jumps in. Quickly the baby tadpoles break from their egg cases to swim off on their own.

The midwife toad, and some other species, make sure of survival by mating three and even four times a year, although most species mate only once.

In Argentina there is one species of frog that lays only a few dozen eggs at a time, but has a very odd and excellent method of protecting its young. Argentineans call it the vaquero, meaning the cowboy, though I don't know why. It's no bigger than a large cricket, and looks vaguely like one. Scientists call it *Rhinoderma darwinii*. The *darwinii* is for Charles Darwin, the great British scientist, who discovered this species as a young man traveling around the world.

After the female vaquero lays her eggs, it is not only the father who protects them. Several other males will join him. Together they stand guard—or maybe it's sit guard—until they know, somehow, that the eggs are close to hatching. This may be two or even three weeks. Then each male picks up several of the eggs with his tongue and tucks them inside his vocal sac.

This vocal sac is huge, considering the size of the male. It is not only under the throat but under the belly and up the sides. Here the eggs hatch into tadpoles and the tadpoles change into frogs about one-half an inch long. Since the adult male is not much over one inch, and may be carrying five or even ten young, he is considerably swollen at this time. Even so, he can still eat and get around. Eventually he opens his mouth and the young vaqueros come bounding out. Then the male, who may or may not have been the father, goes back to his natural size.

Many species of frogs spend practically their entire lives in trees, yet they are as dependent on water for metamorphosis as their earth-bound relatives. Some of them simply climb down

40

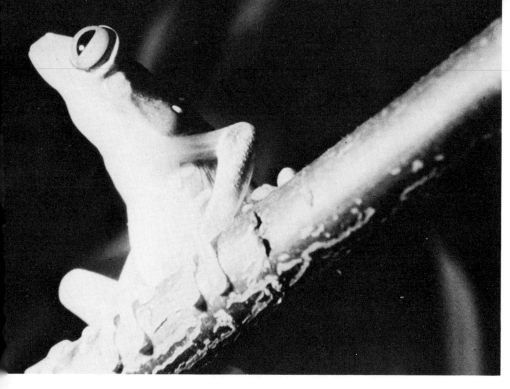

*This Central American tree frog* (Agalychnis callidryas) *spends practically its entire adult life in the treetops. But in the mating season it comes down to where the eggs can be laid in jellylike masses on leaves that hang over pools of water. When the tadpoles hatch, they drop into the water, mature into frogs, and go climbing up the trees. The big pop eyes are a beautiful ruby red with black irises.*

and hop in the water when the time comes to mate. Others have trickier methods. Some of these lay their eggs singly and glue them to a leaf or branch overhanging a pool. Hidden here, they are safe from water bugs, leeches, and other dangers within the pool. Then when the larvae have matured they break from the eggs, tadpoles now, and fall into the water.

In tropical countries where many of the tree frogs live, large air plants grow in the trees. The leaves of many of these form deep cups in which water may stand most of the year. Here some tree frogs lay their eggs to hatch into tadpoles, change into frogs, and never touch the ground at all.

41

# CHAPTER 5

# THE FROG IN SUMMER

When the tadpole absorbs the last of its tail and comes hopping onto land it is, in most ways, a complete frog or toad. It may still grow, a little or a lot, depending on its species. It is not yet sexually mature, but basically it's the same creature it will remain the rest of its life.

It needs food and water.

As mentioned earlier, amphibians cannot live long under very hot, dry conditions. The moisture will evaporate from inside their bodies and they die quickly. This is one reason that most frogs and toads prefer to do their hunting and hopping about at night. During the daylight they usually hide in dark, moist places. In long periods of dry weather they may dig deep into the ground to find moisture and estivate. *Estivation* is practically the same as hibernation, except it is to avoid heat rather than cold.

Despite frogs' great need for water, they cannot drink it. At least, not in the way most animals do. Instead of taking water through its mouth, a frog or toad absorbs it through the skin. So a hop through dew-wet grass is as good as a plunge in a pond.

If the frog does not use its mouth for drinking water, it more than makes up for this when eating. Maybe it would not be correct to call a frog loud-mouthed, because it sings with its mouth closed; but certainly they are big-mouthed. In most species the mouth not only reaches from the front of the face to the eyes but well behind them. When a frog yawns, as they sometimes appear to do, the mouth looks big enough to swallow the rest of the body.

Practically all frogs and toads are insect-eaters. They swallow their prey alive and whole. To help with this some have teeth, and some don't; but these teeth, with rare exceptions, are very small. They are used to help hold a wiggling insect rather than to chew it.

The frog's truly deadly weapon is its tongue. This is not hinged at the back of the mouth, as with human beings, but at the front and stretches back toward the gullet. The tip of the tongue is forked and coated with a sticky substance from glands in the roof of the mouth.

In feeding, the frog uses this tongue like a combination bullwhip and lasso. When some careless insect comes within range, the frog lashes out its tongue with incredible speed. In fact, the

*If the moth stays absolutely still, this leopard frog* (Rana pipiens) *will not recognize it as a possible dinner. But if it flicks a wing the frog can strike as swiftly as a snake.*

tongue moves so fast that it is almost invisible. The forked tip may wrap around the prey or merely stick to it. Then the tongue is pulled back into the mouth, carrying the insect with it. Quite often the captured cricket or butterfly may be almost as big as the frog and too big to be pulled into the mouth all at once. Then the frog uses its hands—without regard for manners —to stuff in anything left over.

But hands, tongue, and teeth are not the only tools a frog uses to help swallow an oversize dinner. It also uses its eyes—and this takes some explaining.

### THE EYES

> . . . the toad, ugly and venomous
> Wears yet a precious jewel in his head.

Shakespeare wrote these lines almost 400 years ago. And few people who have looked carefully at toads and frogs doubt that these creatures have some of the most beautiful eyes in all the animal kingdom. The iris may be bright gold, or silver, or some pastel shade crossed by brilliant, contrasting bars of color. Whatever the color of the individual species' eyes, they will look, as Shakespeare wrote, like precious jewels set in the frog's head.

But basically eyes are to see with rather than be seen. On this score the frog has some advantages over human beings, and some handicaps.

In most frogs the eyes are set wide apart, one on each side of the head, and look in opposite directions. Also, the eyes are raised above the skull. So the frog can see not only in front and to both sides of him, he can see behind and above him as well, all at the same time. On the other hand, he can see most of these things with only one eye at a time. This is called monocular

44

*The bullfrog has large, protruding eyes.*

vision and does not allow as accurate a judgment of distance and shape as binocular vision, where both eyes see the same object at the same time. And if the object is very close to the tip of the frog's snout, he may not be able to see it at all. A bug within one or two inches of a frog's nose is usually completely safe because the frog looks right over it.

Nor do frogs have very good vision at a distance. Those that sit and wait for their food to come close, don't appear to notice anything more than a few feet away. Even bullfrogs and some of the tree frogs that hurl themselves through the air to catch a passing insect will ignore one more than forty or fifty feet away, probably because they don't see it.

Even when the insect is clearly visible, most frogs and toads will not recognize it as a possible dinner unless it moves. A cricket may sit perfectly still within six inches of a frog's nose, and not be touched. If the insect moves slightly, the frog is

45

suddenly alert. If it moves again, the frog's tongue lashes out. And when it strikes, it rarely misses.

On the other hand, some frogs, especially young ones, will try to eat almost anything that moves whether it is living or not. A bullfrog will snap up buckshot or even small marbles rolled past it, one after another.

Nor do a frog's eyes give it a very good idea of size. A baby frog or toad will often tackle an insect as big, or bigger, than itself, and try desperately to swallow it. But as they get older they learn to judge size somewhat better.

The black pupil of the frog's eye goes all the way across the eyeball. The pupil may be horizontal or vertical, depending on the species. At night, when frogs are most active, the pupils may expand until they take up almost the entire eye. This gives the frog better night vision, but men who go hunting for frogs also take advantage of it. Caught in the beam of a flashlight, the frog's eyes will glow like jewels, often a beautiful green. While the light holds steady in its eyes, the frog sits motionless. The hunter can move closer to stab the frog with a gig, or dip it up in a net. But if the light wavers, the frog dives and is gone in an instant.

*Frog hunting with a gig*

Swimming underwater, the frog also has an advantage over human beings. The upper eyelid has no muscles and does not move. But the frog also has two lower lids. One of these, called the nictitating membrane, is transparent. Underwater the frog can pull this over its eye, leaving the other lid open. The nictitating membrane then acts like a skin diver's mask, giving good underwater vision.

And this gets us, at last, to the use of the eyes in eating. The eyes of a frog, as mentioned, stand out well above the skull. But part of the eye also sinks below the skull into the roof of the frog's mouth. When it wishes, the frog can retract its eyes still farther into its mouth. And this helps force an unwilling earthworm or cricket back into the gullet and on to the stomach.

The motion of the eyes is clearly visible. And this is why some persons say a frog bats its eyes while swallowing.

### BREATHING

Frogs have lungs, but no ribs. Nor do they, as a rule, have the muscles that most backboned animals use in breathing. And since there is no separate passage from the frog's nostrils to its lungs, it has to devise some other way of breathing.

To breathe the frog keeps its mouth tightly closed. (This also cuts down on the evaporation of water from its body, which is so important.) Then it lowers the floor of its mouth—a trick that seems to be no problem for a frog. This creates a partial vacuum inside the frog's mouth and sucks air in through the nostrils. Then it closes a valve in the nostrils so the air can't escape and at the same time opens a valve at the rear of the mouth leading into a windpipe. Now it raises the floor of the mouth again— and the air is forced down the windpipe into the lungs. All this gives a bellows-like action to the frog's throat that can be seen plainly.

The Lake Titicaca frog. Note the flaps and folds of skin all over its body, through which it breathes.

It can be truly said that a frog breathes by swallowing air. And since it must do this with its mouth closed, you can suffocate a frog merely by holding its mouth open.

Underwater a frog keeps its nostrils closed and must pop to the surface now and then to breathe. But since a frog sings with both its mouth and nostrils closed, it can, and often does, give an underwater serenade.

There are some frogs that do their breathing in even odder ways. One of these has the wonderful scientific name of *Telmatobius culeus*. It is found in only one place in the world, Lake Titicaca in Bolivia, so we can call it the Lake Titicaca frog.

The lake is a big one, over 3,000 square miles. High in the Andes Mountains, more than 12,000 feet above sea level, it is believed to be the highest navigable lake in the world. And it is loaded with frogs. Jacques Cousteau, a French scientist, has estimated there may be a billion of them. Recently the National Geographic Society sent Dr. Victor Hutchison, of the University of Oklahoma, to Bolivia to study these frogs.

Dr. Hutchison doubts there are a billion Lake Titicaca frogs, but they are probably in the millions. They live not only from one side of the lake to the other, but from the top to the bottom —and the bottom in places is 300 feet down. On the other hand they very rarely come ashore. They are strictly aquatic, breathing underwater. Yet they have no gills—a very strange situation indeed.

Dr. Hutchison learned that the Lake Titicaca frogs lay eggs, just as do most frogs. These hatch into tadpoles, and the tadpoles go through the usual metamorphosis into frogs. Only, it's not quite the usual metamorphosis. The gills of the tadpoles disappear and lungs develop. But these are very weak lungs. Instead of the lungs working to draw air through the nostrils, the Lake Titicaca frog actually breathes through its skin. To do this it needs a lot of skin, and it hangs in flaps and folds from all

49

over the body, especially from the thighs. So the skin takes oxygen from the water and passes it to the blood.

Although the legs of the Titicaca frogs taste like chicken, the Aymara Indians, who live around the lake, do not eat them. Instead, they believe the frogs have medicinal powers, especially for stomach and chest pains. An Indian with a stomachache will cut open a frog and place it on his belly. Sometimes the Indian recovers rapidly—which may or may not have something to do with the frog.

In some parts of West Africa there is a frog that breathes through its hair. Scientifically this may not be exactly correct, since frogs don't have hair. But this one is called the hairy frog and during the breeding season the males do have something that looks like hair along the sides and thighs. These are very fine, threadlike growths much like the gills of the tadpole. The lungs of this hairy frog, like those of the Lake Titicaca frog, are much reduced in size. During the mating season the male apparently needs more oxygen than his lungs can take in, and at this time his "hair" helps with his breathing. The females, like most good frogs, are always bald.

### EARS

If the African hairy frog may be said to breathe with its hair, then the African clawed frog might be said to hear with its hair. But again, this is only partially correct. The African clawed frog, along with a few others—and most fishes—has what is called a lateral line. This is made up of tiny, pitlike organs running along its sides and on its head. In these pits are microscopic hairs that bend with any movement of water along the frog's body. This bending "fires" impulses to the frog's nervous system that tell it which way the water is moving. In this way the frog may hear—or maybe it's feel—the approach of a wading

*The ear—the tympanum—of this little squirrel tree frog may be seen just back of and slightly below the eye. It looks as if it might be a dime just under the skin. Actually, the squirrel tree frog is never more than 1½ inches long.*

bird or some other predator. In fact, so sensitive are these hairs the frog can even detect the movement of small insects and move in to eat rather than be eaten.

Only the clawed frog and a few others have lateral lines. But practically all frogs have ears—only in frogs they are called tympanums—located just behind and slightly below the eye and above the corner of the mouth. Although visible in most species, the tympanum does not stand out from the head as do the ears of many animals. Nor does the tympanum have an external opening. (There is one frog in Siam that has an opening to its ear; but that just proves that among frogs somebody has always got to be different.) Actually, the tympanum is a thin membrane, often with a ridge around it, and usually round or oval. When a sound strikes it, this membrane vibrates, like the eardrum of a human being, and passes the message to the brain.

For some uncertain reason, frogs often react rather oddly to sound. If you approach a pond at night it may sound as if a million frogs are singing at one time. Make a single splashing noise and they are all silent, instantly. Remain quiet, and after awhile, one by one, they begin to sing again. On the other hand, you may sometimes make so much noise approaching a frog that it can't help but hear you—and the frog will simply sit there until you come close enough to be seen. Some naturalists believe that frogs need their eyes to help understand the meaning of sound. Or it may be that, in daylight, the frog feels safe until it sees the danger.

**THE SKIN EATERS**

As mentioned before, tadpoles consume their own tails, even though they don't turn around and bite themselves. But the growing frog is even odder: it literally eats its own skin. Once again this requires some explanation.

The skin of a frog or toad does not grow as the frog grows. So the young frog may quite truly get too big for its britches. It must either change them now and then, or quit growing.

But size is not the only reason a frog often needs to change its skin. Remember, a frog drinks through its skin. The skin helps

*American toad*—Bufo americanus

regulate the body temperature and may help with breathing. Also, as we shall see later, the skin is the anuran's chief method of defense. It has to be kept in good shape, and the frog does this by shedding the old and wearing a new one.

How often a frog sheds depends partially on its age—a young frog sheds more often than an old one—the climate, and the species. It may happen almost every day, or once every ten or so days.

The common toad you see about the yard or garden may shed every three or four days. To do this it starts by yawning—and when this toad yawns its mouth gets every bit as wide as its body. Then it stretches. It humps its back. It shudders. And yawns again. All this loosens the old skin from the new skin beneath it, and the old skin splits down the back.

Now the toad wiggles. It kicks its hind legs. With its hands it rubs furiously at its back and belly, rolling the old skin forward into the corners of its mouth. Still rubbing and swallowing, it pulls the skin forward, like a woman taking a dress off over her head. Only the toad eats the dress as it comes off. The whole process takes only three or four minutes, and there is a fresh, new skin beneath.

A few species change in the water and let the old skin float away, but most eat it. Apparently it contains nutrients the toad needs. Even so, the process seems to leave the toad exhausted. For several minutes it sits and rests, then goes hopping away.


ENEMIES AND DEFENSE

When a frog or toad first changes its skin, the new one has a fresh, shiny look. It doesn't take long, however, hopping around in the mud, for the new skin to look just like the old one. But new skin or old, most frogs can, and often do, change their color.

53

Just how this is done, and even why, is still a bit uncertain. Some naturalists believe frogs change color, chiefly, to match the weather. Light colors reflect heat and dark colors absorb it. Therefore, on a hot, dry day the same frog or toad will be lighter in color than it is on a cool, damp day.

On the other hand, some tropical frogs are brilliantly colored with red and green and yellow at night, then turn a drab gray in daylight. Also many frogs grow pale when singing. The green tree frog gets yellow and the bullfrog that normally is almost black will turn bronze. No one quite knows why.

At least some species also change color in order to camouflage, or hide themselves from enemies. An African clawed frog will turn dark if a dark cloth is spread over the aquarium in which it is living. It will turn pale if a white cloth is placed over it. And if a spotted cloth is put over the aquarium, the frog will become spotted with dark and light. But even without changing, the colors of most frogs help to make them almost invisible. Sitting on a white cloth, a leopard frog is a beautiful mixture of various shades of green, brown, and pale yellows. But against its natural background of green weeds and leaves it seems almost to disappear.

*The leopard frog is one of the most common of North American frogs, found almost everywhere east of the Pacific Coast states. It lives chiefly in swamps and around the edges of ponds.*

*Natives in Central America call this the chicken frog because they say it eats small chickens. Maybe it does, since it grows to be as much as eight inches long. Normally the chicken frog squats on its hind legs. But threatened by a still larger animal, it puffs itself up and raises its rump in an effort to look even bigger than it is.*

Some toads when threatened by a dog or some other animal will puff themselves up and try to look too big to be eaten. Others have a far more realistic defense, and among these are the fire-bellied toads found in Europe. Squatting on the bank of a pond, the fire-belly is a gray, innocent looking, little toad. But let some animal threaten it and the fire-belly straightens its legs, lifts its body from the ground, and rears its head high. This exposes its bright, fire-colored belly—and if the would-be predator is smart, it will leave this little toad alone. This toad's skin secretes a poison that will burn the mouth of any animal that tries to eat it. And if swallowed, it will probably kill its killer.

There are, as we shall see later, many other species of poisonous frogs. Practically all of these are brightly colored, using their colors as a warning to be left alone. But for the non-poisonous frogs, life is one danger after another. Many of the things that threatened the life of tadpoles also threaten the

55

*Of all snakes, the hognose snake is probably the frog's most deadly enemy.*

grown frog. Large fish and wading birds and snakes eat them. Big frogs, such as the bullfrog, eat the smaller ones, including baby bullfrogs. Raccoons, bobcats, and otters find them delicious. And so do men.

Driving through the Everglades National Park I saw an example of how many things can destroy frog life. It was night and suddenly the car lights seemed filled with jumping jewels of all colors. There was water on both sides and apparently every Everglades frog to the north wanted to go south, and everyone to the south was headed north. The car lights gleamed on their bodies, flashed on their eyes, on the drops of water they splashed from the rain-wet road. There were, literally, thousands upon thousands of frogs. It was impossible to drive without killing them by the hundreds.

But it was not automobiles alone that destroyed the frogs. From the mangroves along the side of the road shone the eyes of bobcats and raccoons. Often they came onto the road to get the frogs killed by cars. Snakes slithered on the road and off again. Even night herons were out to join the feast. Yet so many frogs had been killed by cars that the road was littered with them.

I drove back over that same road in the early dawn. The bobcats and raccoons must have eaten their fill, for I saw none. But with the first daylight came the birds: egrets, ibis, herons, and great flocks of crows. By the time the sun came up, the road was clean and there was no sign of the night's slaughter.

Naturalists estimate, remember, that only one frog egg out of twenty will ever become a frog. And they guess—it is only a guess—that no more than one out of ten baby frogs ever live to be a year old. But how long would a frog or toad live if raised safely and fed well?

Nobody knows for sure. There is no record of an individual raised from an egg and kept in captivity until its death of old age. It is known that one toad lived in captivity for 36 years— the Methuselah of all known anurans. But how old it was when captured is uncertain.

Probably, 36 to 40 years is just about as old as any toad could ever get. And toads as a group seem to live longer than frogs. Also, it's possible that a species raised in the north would live longer than one in the south—at least many scientists think so. This is because of the longer period of hibernation in cold climates. At such times the frog remains dormant: it breathes slowly, its heart beats slowly, and possibly it ages slowly.

*This little blue heron is also an enemy of the frog.*

# CHAPTER 6

# JUMPING FROGS

Frogs have long been famous for their ability to jump, and the most famous of all was *The Celebrated Jumping Frog of Calaveras County*. This mighty jumper was the hero of a fiction story by Mark Twain, one of America's greatest writers. According to the story, the frog was owned by a man named Smiley who taught it to jump.

"Why," Mark Twain wrote, "I've seen him set Dan'l Webster down here on this floor—Dan'l Webster was the name of the frog—and sing out, 'Flies, Dan'l, flies!' and quicker'n you could wink he'd spring straight up and snake a fly off'n the counter there, and flop down on the floor ag'in as solid as a gob of mud, and fall to scratching the side of his head with his hind foot as indifferent as if he hadn't no idea he'd been doin' any more'n any frog might do. You never see a frog so modest and straightfor'ard as he was, for all he was so gifted. And when it come to fair and square jumping on a dead level, he could get over more ground at one straddle than any animal of his breed you ever see. Jumping on a dead level was his strong suit. . . ."

According to the story, Dan'l Webster's trainer made a lot of money betting his frog could outjump any other frog in the county. He never lost a bet—until a stranger took advantage of

*This tree frog is not much over an inch long, but it can fly through the air with the greatest of ease. This picure clearly shows that a frog has four joints in its hind legs. This is one reason the frog has such great jumping power.*

a frog's strange habit of gobbling up any moving object that looks like an insect, whether it is or not. This stranger poured Dan'l so full of buckshot, the mighty jumper couldn't get his back end off the floor.

Now, Calaveras County, in California, holds a frog jumping contest every year in honor of Mark Twain's story. And in Capetown, South Africa, there are annual Frogolympics. Stories of some wonderful jumping come out of both places. These stories, like the one by Mark Twain, are sometimes more fiction than fact. On the other hand, scientists have carefully studied the jumping ability of frogs. And some of their findings are as strange as fiction.

Remember that a frog has four joints in its hind legs. It's this that gives it such terrific jumping power. The American bull-

*Note the suction discs at the tips of fingers and toes of this green tree frog which help it climb trees.*

frog is one of the largest of frogs, and one of the best jumpers. A bullfrog that measures eight inches from nose to rump will often jump seventy-two inches—nine times its own length. A five-inch leopard frog can't match the bullfrog's total, but does even better for its size. They have been known to jump thirteen times their length. Among the fairly large species, leopard frogs are the North American champions.

The real champions, however, are to be found in South Africa. One of these is called the arum frog because it normally makes its home inside the bloom of the arum lily. Ivory colored to match the petals of the lily, the frog is thin, streamlined, and never more than an inch long. Inside the lily's bloom it remains perfectly still, almost invisible, until an insect is lured close by the flower's perfume. Then the frog's tongue flicks out, too fast to be visible, and the arum has lunch without seeming to have moved.

If disturbed, the whole frog can move almost as fast as its tongue. A one-inch arum has been measured jumping eighteen inches straight up, and as much as twenty-four inches on the level. Not only that, on the tip of the arum's eight fingers and ten toes (the usual number for most frogs) it has round suction discs. With these it can walk straight up a pane of glass. Or when it hurls itself out of its lily blossom, one finger may touch on a blade of grass or a twig, and stick to it. The frog spins around like a trapeze artist to the far side of the twig—and seems to have vanished in mid-air. (Suction discs on fingers and toes are usual among tree frogs. This gives them the ability not only to climb trees, but to hang upside down on a leaf or blade of grass.)

One South African jumper is even more powerful than the arum frog. It has been known to leap thirty times its own length. If a football player six feet tall could do this, he could take a punt on his own forty yard line, leap into the air, and come down on the other goal line.

At the other extreme is a little one-inch toad called Rose's toad. With its mightiest effort, it can hop just about one inch. On the other hand, it can run like a mouse, and almost as fast.

Not long ago a group of scientists set out to study the jumping ability of an American bullfrog. In a laboratory they set up a pond for the frog to dive into. They brought flies and crickets for the frog to jump after. They set up a whole battery of high speed cameras to record the event. And carefully they put the frog down on a rock beside the pond.

The frog sat there. A scientist nudged its rear end, but it did not move. Someone tied a cricket on a string and swung it past the frog's nose. It did not move. The cameramen waited.

The frog jumped. It moved so fast the pictures showed the place where the frog had been, but nothing else.

The scientists rigged up a small electric wire and sat the frog

*An American bullfrog*

on it. The cameras were synchronized with the wire. The frog got a light shock—and soared into the air while the cameras took twenty pictures every second, each picture taking only twenty-five millionth of a second.

Working in this way the scientists learned that when the frog jumped, it first retracted its eyes as it would do underwater. It raised the third lid—the nictitating membrane—which protected the eye but still allowed vision. When it took off, the arms hung limp at the sides but the legs stretched straight out. Then, just before hitting the water, the frog raised its arms over its head just as a human diver would do.

The whole jump usually took less than half a second.

The electric shock would send the frog leaping whenever the scientists wanted. But this was a jump of surprise, not one aimed at a passing insect. And the scientists wanted to study exactly how the frog caught its food.

A beam of light was passed just over the frog's head. Now, when the frog jumped, it would break this beam. The automatic cameras were synchronized to go into action when the beam was broken. Then a hungry bullfrog was placed on its rock and a cricket swung past on a string.

In this way it was learned that a frog jumping for food lowered its eyes and raised the nictitating membrane just as it did diving into water. In the first part of the jump the arms hung limp. If the frog's aim was absolutely accurate, it lost sight of the target as it came close: with its eyes retracted, it could see nothing close to its nose. But if its aim was off in the slightest, then one eye or the other could see. The frog twisted in mid-air, and practically never missed.

### HOW SMART ARE FROGS?

When a toad awakes in the spring from its long winter nap and starts looking for water in which to mate and lay eggs, how does it know which way to go? No one can say for sure, but most naturalists believe it is instinct and not memory. Certainly it is instinct that teaches the young frog, facing its first winter, to search out some safe place and hibernate. The frog does this alone, with no one to teach it. It is instinct that tells the bullfrog to mate and leave its eggs in water, and tells the midwife toad to carry the eggs wrapped around its body.

Most naturalists believe that toads are a little more intelligent than most frogs. But not even toads win intelligence prizes. On the other hand, they are capable of learning, and remembering, the things they truly need to know. And most of these deal with food.

At the Archbold Biological Station in Florida a team of scien-

*This is the southern toad,* Bufo terrestris, *a common garden-type toad in the southeast. Most herpetologists believe toads are more intelligent than frogs.*

tists took a hungry young toad and held a robber fly on a string in front of it. The toad gobbled up the fly happily. Then the scientists swung a bumblebee in front of the toad. The bumblebee looks almost exactly like the robber fly; but the bumblebee carries a vicious stinger which the robber fly does not. The young toad had never seen a bumblebee, and grabbed it instantly. The bee stung the toad.

The toad went almost straight into the air. It spit out the bee and came down backing away.

Now the scientists took another robber fly and passed it in front of the toad. The toad put its head down and its hands up.

It would have absolutely none of the fly.

To prove that this was because the toad had learned to avoid anything that looked like a bumblebee and not because it was no longer hungry, the scientists next used a dragonfly. The toad immediately ate it.

If a toad in captivity is fed in a certain place at a certain time of the day, it will learn the place and time, and be there, waiting for its food. On the other hand, I've seen a tree frog sitting on a windowpane trying to catch insects on the other side. It kept flicking its tongue against the pane. And though this may have been my imagination, I could swear it looked dumbfounded that it never caught a bug.

CHAPTER 7

# THE STRANGE
# AND UNUSUAL

Travelers in western Africa often heard native stories about a giant frog. But just how big this frog was, no one seemed to agree. Some said it was as big as a chicken, and some said it was big enough to eat chickens. Some said it contained a poison so deadly it would kill a man just to touch it, and some said it was good to eat. There was not even any real agreement on where these monsters lived. However, most of the stories mentioned the rain forest just north of the equator. In 1966 the National Geographic Society sent Dr. Paul Zahl to search for the world's biggest frog.

Dr. Zahl had no trouble hearing stories about the frog. But it took a long while to find a native who said he knew where to find them. With this man as guide, the expedition set out into the rain forest.

The guide told Dr. Zahl that natives called the giant frog "niamona," which meant "mother's son." This was because the frog looked somewhat like, and was as big as, a newborn child. It lived beside rivers that rushed over rocks and waterfalls, and would sit for hours where the spray kept it wet. It had very keen ears and was hard to approach, but if it had a voice no one had ever heard it.

Days later, deep in the rain forest, Dr. Zahl saw his first giant frog. He was some distance away, and for a long while he studied it carefully through field glasses. The frog was a monster; at this distance he could not tell just how big. It sat on a rock in the river, just below a waterfall.

Carefully Dr. Zahl set up his camera with telescopic lens. But before he could take a picture there was a sound, a movement—he could not be sure what. With one giant leap the frog flashed through the air and into the river.

Not long afterward the explorers found another frog, seated like the first on a rock in the river. Leaving Dr. Zahl and the others to watch, their guide circled carefully through the trees and slipped into the river behind the frog. Quietly he waded toward it, carrying a long bamboo pole with a heavy line and fishhook on the end. Dr. Zahl kept expecting the frog to jump into the river, but it did not. Later he would learn that this frog, unlike some others, could not see behind it.

When he was close enough, the native lowered his pole over the frog's back. If the hook touched the frog, there was no sign. When the hook slid between the frog's haunches and its body, the native heaved back. The hook bit into the frog's leg and jerked it high in the air.

Before the expedition left Africa, several other giant frogs were captured alive. They weighed as much as seven pounds, and measured nearly a yard long from nose to toes. The head was as broad as a saucer, and the arms almost as thick as a man's wrist. On the tips of the toes and fingers were suction pads that helped the frogs hold to the slippery rocks on which they liked to sit.

Dr. Zahl learned that different African tribes regarded the big frogs in different ways. Some thought they were sacred and not to be harmed. Pygmy tribes, however, thought they were delicious and to be eaten whenever possible.

Except for their great size, these frogs (they now go by the scientific name of *Rana goliath*) were much like the American bullfrog. The females laid eggs that hatched into tadpoles. The tadpoles went through a metamorphosis into frogs. And at this stage they not only looked like bullfrogs, they were about the same size. But the bullfrog quits growing when it reaches a length of twelve to seventeen inches, head to toe. *Rana goliath* just keeps on growing.

### FLYING AND FIGHTING

Goliath is the biggest of all known frogs, but other species are even stranger in different ways. Consider the flying frogs of South America and Asia.

Technically, these frogs don't really fly. Nor is it just a jump either. If it were, then the arum frog, one of the champion jumpers, couldn't hold the tape measure to *Hyla venulosa*, a moderately good jumper.

The flying frogs are actually gliders. They spend most of their lives in the treetops, feeding on passing insects. If one sees an insect three feet or so away it leaps after it, apparently without regard for what is below and beyond. With the insect in its mouth, the flying frog may touch a twig with a finger or toe, and stick to it like the arum. Or it may find itself with nothing but space below. If so, it spreads its webbed fingers and toes—long and heavily webbed for its size—to form wings. Then it glides gently down to earth, forty or fifty feet from where it started.

In a South American jungle a flying frog may use its gliding ability to escape a monkey or some other treetop predator. But on the ground it may come face to face with another enemy of an entirely different type—a horned frog.

There are several species of horned frogs. And most of them, as the South American Indians say, are ugly and mean as the

68

devil, from whom they get their horns. Actually, the horns are neither dangerous nor real horns. In most species they are merely part of the eyelids, and though they look hard and sharp, they're not. But the frogs themselves are truly ugly and mean.

Some species are no more than an inch long, and some are huge, eight-inch fellows. Big or little, they have tremendous mouths for their size, sharp teeth, and they will bite just about anything that moves, including the hand that feeds them; many a herpetologist has had his or her fingers nipped while feeding a captive horned frog. While most frogs hop away from danger if given a chance, horned frogs will turn to face and fight it. Try to come up behind a horned frog and instead of jumping away, it will swing around and glare at you.

Argentine cowboys believe that a horse bitten on the lip while grazing by a horned frog will die of poison. Actually, the horned frogs are not poisonous. It is true, however, that they are mean and brave enough to bite a horse. They will also bite and

*A horned frog of South America*

try to swallow frogs that are truly poisonous. In this case the horned frog is lucky if it can spit out its prey and learn to leave such things alone. (Remember the toad that tried to eat the bumblebee?)

As fighters the horned frogs of South America have a rival that lives only on the island of Okinawa and is called the dagger frog. Unlike most frogs, the dagger frog has a thumb. This is actually a short, sharp bone covered by very thin skin. If picked up, the dagger frog will wrap both arms around the man's hand and stab with its thumb. It **can** do this hard enough to bring blood.

Both the horned frogs and the dagger frog can make you go *Ouch!* but they are not really dangerous. There are frogs, however, that are truly deadly.

# CHAPTER 8

# SMALL, BEAUTIFUL,
# AND DEADLY

Deep in a South American jungle Dr. Marte Latham was skin-ning a tiny black-and-yellow frog. She had killed it very care-fully with ether, and now, using surgical scissors, she slit the skin along the belly. As she did so the scissors slipped, and one point pricked her finger where it touched the frog. It was a small wound, barely enough to bring a few drops of blood—but it was also enough to allow the most minute bit of poison to enter. Almost immediately she felt as though an iron hand were choking her.

Dr. Latham had come to South America to study a group of frogs called the poison arrow frogs. Now it flashed through her mind that she was learning about this poison in a way she had never intended. Quickly she squeezed the injured finger to cut off the circulation. She began to suck out the blood, but the choking sensation seemed to have paralyzed the muscles of her throat. Her chest hurt and she gasped for breath.

For several minutes Dr. Latham thought she was going to die. Then, gradually, the sickness passed. Within two hours she felt normal again. But she'd had a dramatic lesson in how deadly the poison of some frogs can be.

71

This is a poison arrow frog from Central and South America. It is only one-half inch long, but its body contains poison enough to kill twenty or more of the animals big enough to eat it.

This poison arrow frog is neither playing dead nor taking a morning sunbath. Like the fire-bellied toads of Europe, this one is bright red on the underside. When danger threatens, it doesn't try to jump away. Instead, it rolls over to expose the red warning color.

*This horned frog from South America has made the mistake of trying to eat a poison arrow frog. It has spit the frog out, but is now holding its mouth open trying to cool the burning pain.*

In Central and South America there are many species of poison arrow frogs. Most of them are small, rarely more than two inches long, and brightly colored. Where the coloring of most frogs and toads helps to make them able to hide from enemies, the poison arrow frogs seem to flaunt their gaudy colors. Most naturalists believe that this, like the stomach color of the fire-bellied toads, is a protective device. Any animal that has once tried to eat a poison arrow frog is not likely to try again, even if it lives to have the chance.

Indeed, except for man, the poison arrow frogs have almost no enemies. And it is this same poison that makes them attractive to the South American Indians. Long before Columbus they had learned to use this poison to tip their darts and hunting arrows.

73

To do this, the Indians first capture the little frogs by hand. This is perfectly safe, so long as the Indian does not have a cut or open sore because the poison must enter the bloodstream to be effective. Even so, if held for any length of time, the frog may cause a painful rash. So the Indians catch the frogs by hand, but carry them rolled in leaves.

Just how the Indians first learned to get the poison from the frogs is unknown, but scientists now understand how this works. All frogs and toads have glands in the skin. These secrete a fluid that keeps the skin moist and pliable. But along with these glands some species have other glands that create poison. In many toads the parotid gland, a roundish disc just back of the eye, is clearly visible. When roughly handled, as when caught by some other animal, these parotid glands give off a milky poison. In only a few species is this as deadly as with the poison arrow frogs. But often it is enough to make a dog or cat quickly drop its would-be dinner.

In the poison arrow frogs these glands are scattered all about the body. But like the toad, they work only when roughly handled. And they will function even after the frog is dead. So the Indians kill the frog with a pointed stick, then hold its body over a slow fire. As the frog grows hotter, the glands create their poison. And the Indians rub the tips of their arrows along the frog's body. Dr. Latham watched Indians poison as many as fifty darts from the body of one frog no more than one and one-fourth inches long. When shot into a bird or monkey, these darts caused almost instant death.

It is not necessary to go to South America to find poison frogs. Many of those seen hopping about gardens in the United States and Canada create some poisons of their own. None are as deadly as their southern relatives, but some are poisonous enough to make such natural enemies as dogs and foxes leave them alone.

74

One of the best at defending itself is the Colorado River toad. This is a big, warty-looking, broad-backed toad that lives not only near the Colorado River but throughout a good bit of the southwest. In a semidesert country, this toad often makes its home beneath the water tanks of cattle. Or it may be seen at night under the street lights of small towns. Sometimes a dozen or more will gather under a single light, snapping up the moths that flutter past.

If a dog or coyote attacks, the Colorado River toad is too slow to escape by hopping away or digging into the ground. Instead, its glands put out a thickish fluid that burns the mouth of its attacker. This burning seems to be almost instantaneous, and usually the animal spits out the toad as quickly as possible. But the Colorado River toad has been known to kill a full-grown German shepherd dog that swallowed it.

The marine toad, or giant toad, is even bigger than the Colo-

*The giant or marine toad, Bufo marinus. If a dog should happen on this gathering, it had best eat the dog food and leave the toads alone. These toads are deadly poison to dogs. They are harmless to human beings, but if handled, don't rub your eyes before washing your hands.*

rado River toad, and just as capable of looking after itself. The poison its parotid glands secretes tends to stop the heart of any animal that swallows it. On the other hand, both the marine and Colorado River toads may be safely handled without causing warts or any other problem. Just be sure to wash your hands before rubbing your eyes or touching your mouth. Otherwise you may learn the hard way why a dog will drop these toads in such a hurry.

One of the most common frogs in the United States is the pickerel frog. A brown or greenish frog with dark spots, it looks almost exactly like another common frog, the leopard frog. But there is a strange difference. Hunters collecting live frogs for sale have sometimes put various species in a bag together; a little later they have found all the frogs dead except for one pickerel frog.

Obviously, the pickerel frog is poisonous to other frogs, but why this should be, no one seems to know. And certainly it is not poisonous to birds or fish: the name pickerel frog comes from the fact that fishermen often use it as bait for pickerel and other fish. Indeed, the legs of practically all frogs are both safe and good to eat after the skin has been removed.

CHAPTER **9**

# THE FRIENDS OF MAN

In the laboratory of a large medical college doctors took a tiny bit of skin from the back of a baby frog. Then they took a bit of skin from the belly of this same frog. The skin from the back was grafted on the frog's belly, and the skin from the belly was grafted on its back.

As the frog grew and shed its skin from time to time, the light-colored belly skin stayed light, even though it was on the back. And the dark-colored skin from the back stayed dark, sur-rounded by the light belly skin.

From this the doctors learned that there was a chemical dif-ference in the skin itself, and that this difference remained, even though the location of the skin had changed.

Next the experiment was carried a step farther. The skin grafts had been made on a baby frog before the nerve ends grew out to contact the skin. After these nerve ends were grown, the doctors took a feather and tickled the frog on the patch of dark skin grafted to its belly. With a sudden kick of its leg, the frog scratched its back. When the light skin on the back was tickled, the frog scratched its belly.

There was only one conclusion: something in the skin itself told the nerve, "I am a piece of belly skin," even though it was now on the frog's back.

Thousands of experiments of this kind have been conducted on frogs throughout the world's laboratories. Teen-age students taking their first course in zoology study the frog. Some of the world's most highly skilled scientists work with frogs. In practically every university and medical school the frog plays a tremendous role in the ever-continuing education of scientists.

The reason is simple. The frog's entire life, from a transparent egg fertilized outside the female's body, through the tadpole metamorphosis to adult frog, may be easily seen and studied. It is the only naked vertebrate where this is true.

Dr. George Nace, Director of the Center for Human Growth and Development at the University of Michigan, wrote that "Almost every major feature of the human body is represented in the frog. . . . There is hardly an area of biology or medicine that has not been made richer by the work done with the frog as the research animal." Experiments that may lead toward the control of cancer and problems of the human nervous system

*Many frogs are used in school science courses.*

are being conducted around the world with frogs. When Dr. Marte Latham worked with the poison arrow frogs of South America she collected the venom in test tubes. These were sent to laboratories in the United States. Now work with this poison promises to help in controlling the heart attacks of human beings.

But the frog's passive role in modern laboratories is not the only way in which it has helped mankind. For thousands of years the frog and toad have been a friend of farmers. Hopping about a garden or farm, they consume vast numbers of insects— and without the pollution caused by modern insecticides. It has been estimated that one toad is worth about fifty dollars a year to a farmer.

In some cases it may be worth even more. The giant toad, once found only in South America, was taken to the United States, Hawaii, Puerto Rico, practically everywhere sugar cane is grown. There it happily munches on beetles that would otherwise munch on the cane.

When you put a spoonful of sugar in your iced tea, be thankful to the giant toad. And if you must go to a doctor, you can be thankful to many frogs for helping that doctor know what to do.

79

African clawed frog, 29, 30, 50
*Agalychnis callidryas*, 41
American toad, 24, 52
Amphibians, 9, 10, 14, 15, 17 ff., 37, 42
Amplexus, 23
Animal pole, 25
Anura, 14, 15, 37, 53
Archbold Biological Station, 63
Arum frog, 60, 68
Atheneau, 16
Barking frog, 38
Barking tree frog, 16, 21, 38
Bladderwort, 36
*Bufo americanus*, 52
*Bufo marinus*, 15, 75
*Bufo terrestris*, 64
Bullfrog, 15, 19, 24, 25, 31 f., 34 f., 45 f.,
    56, 59 f., 61 ff., 68
Caecilian, 14
Caudata, 14
Chicken frog, 55
Colorado River toad, 75 f.
Cousteau, Jacques, 49
Cricket frog, 20, 21
Dagger frog, 70
Darwin, Charles, 40
Devonian Period, 9
Egg tooth, 38
Estivation, 42
Everglades National Park, 56
Fire-bellied toad, 55, 72
Florida gopher frog, 20
Giant toad, 75
Giant water bug, 36
Greenhouse frog, 37 ff.
Green tree frog, 21
Gynmophiona, 14
Hairy frog, 50
Hibernation, 17, 42
Hognose snake, 56
Horned frog, 68 ff., 73
Hutchison, Victor, 49

*Hyla cinerea*, 21
*Hyla crucifer*, 20
*Hyla gratiosa*, 16
*Hyla venulosa*, 68
Lake Titicaca frog, 48 ff.
Latham, Marte, 71, 74, 79
Leopard frog, 43, 54
*Macbeth*, 12
Metamorphosis, 28, 30 ff., 37 f., 40, 49
Midwife toad, 39 f.
Nace, George, 78
National Geographic Society, 49, 66
Opercular fold, 29
Paradoxical frog, 34 f.
Pickerel frog, 76
Pig frog, 19, 20, 23
Pine woods tree frog, 20
Poison arrow frog, 71 ff.
Polliwog, 26
Pollution, 36
*Rana catesbeiana*, 15
*Rana goliath*, 68
*Rana grylio*, 19
*Rana pipiens*, 43
*Rhinoderma darwinii*, 40
Rose's toad, 61
Salamander, 14
Salientia, 14, 15
Shakespeare, 12, 44
Southern toad, 64
Spadefoot toad, 32 ff.
Spiracle, 29
Spiraculum, 29
Spring peeper, 20, 21
Surinam toad, 38 f.
Tadpole, 26–42, 52, 68
*Telmatobius culeus*, 49
Twain, Mark, 58, 59
Vaquero frog, 40
Vegetable pole, 25, 38
Warts, 14
    superstition about, 12
Zahl, Paul, 66 f.